DIVORCE

DECODED

The Professional Man's Guide to
Divorce and Custody in New York

ASIA SCARLETT-JONES

Neither the author nor the publisher assumes any responsibility or liability whatsoever on behalf of the consumer or reader of this material. Any per-ceived slight of any individual or organization is purely unintentional.

The resources in this book are provided for informational purposes only and should not be used to replace the specialized training and professional judgment of a health care or mental health care professional.

Neither the author nor the publisher can be held responsible for the use of the information provided within this book. Please always consult a trained professional before making any decision regarding the treatment of yourself or others.

For more information, email asia@asjlawoffice.com

DISCLAIMER

In this book, all names of individuals, events,
and places mentioned have been altered to protect privacy
and confidentiality. Any resemblance to real people, living or
deceased, or actual locations is purely coincidental.

DEDICATION

To the father whose journey I could only witness from the sidelines during my law school days — your struggle touched my heart and ignited a fierce commitment within me to advocate for parental rights. Although I was not yet equipped to offer the legal assistance you needed then, your story has shaped my career and this book. I hope that the insights contained herein can serve as a guide for many others to achieve the justice that was so elusive in your case. May this work honor your enduring love and dedication to your child.

TABLE OF CONTENTS

FOREWORD

WRITTEN BY JAYDEN DOYÉ, CPA

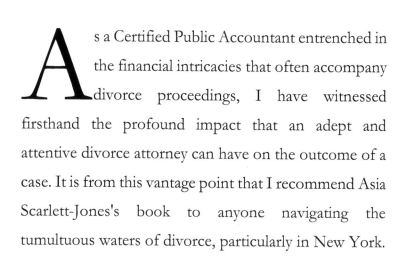

As a Certified Public Accountant entrenched in the financial intricacies that often accompany divorce proceedings, I have witnessed firsthand the profound impact that an adept and attentive divorce attorney can have on the outcome of a case. It is from this vantage point that I recommend Asia Scarlett-Jones's book to anyone navigating the tumultuous waters of divorce, particularly in New York.

Asia Scarlett-Jones is not just a seasoned attorney; she embodies a rare blend of legal insight, empathy, and strategic thinking that sets her apart in family law. Her insights throughout this book are grounded in robust legal expertise and enriched by her comprehensive understanding of the human elements in divorce cases. This dual perspective is invaluable, as the decisions made during a divorce can have long-lasting financial and emotional consequences.

I have observed her unwavering dedication to her client's best interests. She is keen to navigate complex legal and financial landscapes, ensuring her clients are well informed and prepared for each step of the process. This book extends that guidance to its readers, providing them with a roadmap through the legal, emotional, and financial aspects of divorce.

Asia's approach to client relationships is particularly noteworthy. She fosters a communicative and transparent relationship, which is crucial during such a critical time. Her commitment to educating her clients, as illustrated in this book, empowers them to make informed decisions that benefit their long-term well-being.

For those facing the daunting prospect of divorce, understanding your rights and options is imperative. This book is an essential resource, offering clarity and guidance through Asia's expert lens. Whether you are in the early stages of considering a divorce or deep in the throes of legal proceedings, Asia's insights can provide you with the tools necessary to navigate this challenging process with greater confidence and control.

I can assert without reservation that Asia Scarlett-Jones's book is a pivotal read for anyone involved in or facing a divorce. Her expertise, coupled with a genuine concern for her clients, makes this book a beacon for those seeking not only to survive their divorce but to emerge with their dignity and finances intact.

Divorce Decoded

INTRODUCTION

Welcome to *The Professional Man's Guide to Divorce and Custody in New York*, a comprehensive guide designed to help you navigate the often-tumultuous waters of divorce and custody battles, tailored for men in the finance sector. As you may already know, divorce can be a complex and challenging journey, laced with legal intricacies, financial complications, and emotional turbulence. This book aims to be your trusted companion through this difficult phase, offering clarity, strategy, and support.

As a professional in the finance sector, you may be accustomed to dealing with high-stakes situations and intricate financial dealings. However, when it comes to divorce and custody, the stakes are personal, and the complexities extend beyond balance sheets and portfolios. New York's family law system presents its own rules and challenges; navigating this system requires legal expertise and an understanding of its impact on your personal and professional life.

Throughout this guide, you will find detailed, step-by-step information covering every aspect of divorce and custody in New York. This book covers everything from understanding the basics of New York family law, managing financial considerations before and during a divorce, and strategies for asset protection and equitable distribution. We delve into high-net-worth divorces, dealing with international assets, and corporate structures, and provide essential insights on child custody and support.

Moreover, this book is not just about legal procedures and financial strategies. It's about understanding your rights, evaluating your options, and making informed decisions that safeguard your interests and those of your loved ones. It's about emerging from a divorce not only unscathed but well-positioned for the future.

Whether you are contemplating a divorce, in the midst of one, or seeking to understand your situation post-divorce better, this book is your resource. It's written to empower you with knowledge, equip you with strategies, and encourage you to face this challenging phase with confidence and foresight.

Remember, while divorce marks the end of a marriage, it's also the beginning of a new phase of your life. With the right guidance and approach, you can navigate this transition effectively and lay the foundations for a prosperous and fulfilling future.

Welcome to your journey through understanding and mastering the intricacies of divorce and custody in New York.

PREFACE

As a divorce attorney practicing in the vibrant yet often unforgiving landscape of New York City, I have witnessed the emotional and financial upheavals that divorce can bring into people's lives. I was compelled to write this book, through this lens of personal experience and professional dedication. My goal is to demystify the complexities of the divorce process and to offer guidance that empowers individuals to navigate their proceedings with clarity and confidence.

The genesis of this book lies in the countless consultations and cases I have handled over the years. Each client brought a unique story, a different challenge, and a personal journey that required legal expertise, compassion, and understanding. I realized that while every divorce is distinct, the confusion and anxiety surrounding the process are nearly universal. This book aims to address those concerns by shedding light on the key aspects of divorce—from understanding one's rights and obligations to making informed decisions about child custody, spousal support, and asset division.

In these pages, you will find a comprehensive guide through the stages of divorce, illuminated by anecdotes from my practice to provide real-world examples of how various issues can be resolved. I discuss the importance of choosing the right attorney, the intricacies of negotiating settlements, and the critical aspects of post-divorce adjustments. This book also explores the emotional journey of divorce, offering insights into navigating this life transition with resilience.

The writing of this book was also influenced by my interactions with other professionals in related fields, such as financial advisors and mental health experts, whose perspectives enrich the discussions on how to handle the broader impacts of divorce.

I hope that this book serves as a valuable resource for anyone facing the prospect of divorce. Whether you are just starting to consider your options or are in the midst of proceedings, the information provided here aims to give you the tools needed to proceed with confidence and to make decisions that are best for your future.

Thank you for turning to this book in your time of need. May the insights within these pages provide you with clarity and courage as you move forward on your journey.

Divorce Decoded

Chapter 1

Introduction to New York Family Law and Divorce

New York family law encompasses a wide range of legal issues related to familial relationships, including marriage, divorce, child custody, support, and adoption. It is governed by statutes, case law, and judicial precedent that shape the legal landscape for families across the state.

Central to New York family law is the concept of equitable distribution, which governs the division of marital property upon divorce. Unlike community property states, where marital assets are divided equally, New York employs a system of equitable distribution, which aims to divide assets fairly and considers various factors such as each spouse's contributions to the marriage, earning capacity, and financial needs.

Additionally, New York recognizes various grounds for divorce, including fault-based grounds such as adultery, abandonment, and cruelty, as well as no-fault grounds, where the marriage has irretrievably broken down for a specified period.

The divorce process in New York typically begins with the filing of a Summons and Complaint or Summons with Notice with the appropriate court. From there, the parties navigate a series of legal procedures and court appearances, including the exchange of financial information, negotiation of settlement terms, and, if necessary, litigation in court.

It's important to note that New York offers both contested and uncontested divorce options. In an **uncontested divorce**, the parties agree on all issues related to the divorce, including division of assets, child custody, and support, and submit a written agreement to the court for approval. In a **contested divorce**, where the parties are unable to settle, the court will intervene to resolve disputed issues through litigation.

Throughout the divorce process, parties may also engage in alternative dispute resolution methods such as mediation or collaborative law, which offer opportunities to resolve conflicts outside the courtroom more amicably and cost-effectively.

One of the most critical aspects of navigating the divorce process in New York is securing competent legal representation. A skilled attorney specializing in family law can provide invaluable guidance, advocacy, and support throughout every stage of the proceedings.

From ensuring that your rights are protected to advocating for your best interests in negotiations or court hearings, an experienced attorney will be your strongest ally in achieving a favorable outcome. Also, your legal representation will help alleviate the stress and burden of finding your way through complex legal procedures, allowing you to focus on rebuilding your life during this challenging transition.

CHAPTER 2

FINANCIAL PREPARATION BEFORE FILING FOR DIVORCE

A s you embark on the journey of divorce, financial preparation is key to ensure you have a smooth and equitable process. Here, I will guide you through the essential steps of gathering financial documents, assessing assets and liabilities, and understanding the financial implications of divorce.

Before initiating divorce proceedings, it's crucial to gather all relevant financial documents. These may include bank statements, tax returns, pay stubs, retirement account statements, investment portfolios, mortgage documents, and any other financial records pertinent to your marriage.

Gathering these documents early on will not only streamline the divorce process but also provide a clear and comprehensive picture of your financial situation. By having all of the necessary documentation in hand, you'll be better prepared to negotiate a fair division of assets and liabilities and ensure that your financial interests are protected.

Once you've gathered all financial documents, the next step will be to assess all of your assets and liabilities. This will involve identifying and accurately valuing all marital assets, including but not limited to, real estate, vehicles, investments, business interests, and personal property. You will also need to determine any marital debts or liabilities, such as mortgages, loans, and credit card debt.

Assessing your assets and liabilities is critical for equitable distribution; it provides a basis for determining each spouse's financial standing and contribution to the marriage. By conducting a thorough assessment, you'll be better equipped to advocate for your fair share of marital property and ensure that debts are divided equitably.

Divorce can also have significant financial implications that extend far beyond the division of assets and liabilities. This is why it's essential to understand the financial ramifications of divorce and how it may impact your future financial security. For example, you'll need to consider the tax consequences of asset division, alimony payments, and child support obligations. In addition, you may need to reassess your budget and financial goals post-divorce, taking into account changes in income, expenses, and lifestyle.

Moreover, divorce could also necessitate updates to estate planning documents, beneficiary designations, and other legal arrangements to reflect your new circumstances.

When understanding the financial implications of divorce, you can plan for the future and mitigate any potential challenges or uncertainties that may arise.

When I first embarked on my journey as a divorce attorney, I realized the crucial role of financial preparation. At my firm, we use a client portal to streamline the collection of necessary financial documents. It's the backbone of the divorce process, beginning with the comprehensive statement of net worth required by the court. This document necessitates a thorough collection of bank statements, pension plans, and other assets pertinent to equitable distribution.

We instruct clients to systematically upload their documents into designated folders within the portal. This meticulous organization not only aids in preparing the financial statement for the court but also provides us with a comprehensive overview of the client's financial standing. It's essential to differentiate between what constitutes separate and marital property early in the process, which is why these documents are so vital.

Most people do not maintain thorough records of their financial affairs, making this stage often the longest and the most emotionally taxing. For those who have been in long-term marriages, gathering financial information for decades can feel overwhelming. This introspection into one's financial contributions to the marriage is emotional, especially for clients who are defendants in the divorce—they did not choose this upheaval.

To mitigate the emotional toll, we maintain weekly check-ins with our clients to support them through this process. However, complications arise when full disclosure is not met.

For instance, I once represented a client, let's call her "Client Blue," who was significantly less informed about the family's finances compared to her husband, a hedge fund manager. Her lack of financial awareness was a severe handicap when it came to equitable distribution.

Throughout their marriage, her husband managed all financial aspects, from luxurious trips to handling all marital debt through his accounts. He even purchased properties without her knowledge. As the divorce proceedings began, it became apparent that he had manipulated and obscured assets. Our team faced a daunting task in tracing these hidden assets, which involved subpoenaing numerous financial entities to uncover the true extent of his financial maneuvers.

Despite the challenges, we were able to trace significant investments and properties, including a home bought in cash in Texas. This discovery was crucial in ensuring that Client Blue received her fair share of the marital assets. The case underscored the importance of thorough financial preparation and vigilance in divorce proceedings, a principle that guides our approach to supporting our clients through these challenging times.

Divorce Decoded

CHAPTER 3

LEGAL CONSIDERATIONS AND COSTS IN DIVORCE

As you navigate the divorce process, understanding the various legal considerations and associated costs is essential for making informed decisions and proper planning. In this chapter, we'll explore the different types of divorce available in New York, discuss legal fees and expenses, and provide practical guidance on budgeting for legal costs.

In New York, there are several types of divorce proceedings available, each with its own set of requirements and implications:

» *Uncontested Divorce-* Sarah and John, a married couple have decided to end their marriage amicably. They've reached an agreement on asset division, child custody, and support arrangements. Sarah and John opt for an *uncontested divorce,* where they submit a written agreement to the court outlining the terms of their divorce. This type of divorce typically involves less time and expense compared to contested divorces.

» *Contested Divorce-* Now, consider Lisa and David, who are unable to agree on key issues such as asset division and child custody. Despite their best efforts to negotiate, they found themselves at an impasse. Lisa files for a *contested divorce, and the case proceeds to litigation in court. The judge will ultimately decide on disputed matters, which can prolong the divorce process and increase legal expenses.*

» ***No-Fault Divorce-*** Emily and Michael have grown apart over the years and no longer wish to remain married. They decide to pursue a no-fault divorce, citing irreconcilable and irretrievable differences as the grounds for their separation. *In a no-fault divorce, there's no need to prove fault or wrongdoing on either party's part, simplifying the legal process and reducing conflict.*

» ***Fault-Based Divorce-*** Contrastingly, let's consider Jack and Amanda's marriage that has been marred by infidelity. Amanda decides to file for a *fault-based divorce*, alleging adultery as the grounds for dissolution. *Fault-based divorces require evidence to support the allegations, which can complicate proceedings and lead to heightened conflict between the parties.*

27

Understanding the differences between these types of divorce will help you determine the most appropriate course of action for your unique situation and guide your decision-making process moving forward.

Legal fees and expenses are an inevitable part of the divorce process, making it essential that you understand what to expect in terms of costs. These may include attorney fees, court filing fees, and fees for expert witnesses or appraisers, and other related expenses.

The cost of legal representation can vary depending on factors such as the complexity of the case, the attorney's experience and expertise, and the need for additional services or expert testimony. It's important to discuss fee structures and payment arrangements with your attorney upfront to ensure transparency and avoid unpleasant surprises down the line.

Budgeting for legal costs may need to be considered when preparing for divorce. Start by estimating the potential expenses associated with your case, including attorney fees, court costs, and any additional services or resources you may need. Consider your financial resources and determine how much you can afford to allocate towards your legal representation. You may even need to prioritize certain expenses or explore alternative funding options, such as payment plans or financing arrangements, to cover the costs of your divorce.

Creating a budget and financial plan for legal costs can help you manage expenses and ensure that you're adequately prepared for the financial implications of divorce.

Navigating the intricate landscape of divorce law in New York requires a strategic approach, especially when it concerns high-net-worth individuals.

As a divorce attorney serving a professional clientele, I've encountered numerous cases where the financial stakes and legal strategies must be balanced to secure the best outcomes for my clients.

One such case involved a client who, as the moneyed spouse, faced significant risks in a contested divorce scenario. Understanding the nuances of no-fault versus fault-based divorces in New York, we opted for a no-fault uncontested divorce. This strategy is not only favored by judges but also lessens the adversarial process. Proving grounds in a "fault divorce," such as infidelity, rarely impacts the financial outcome but significantly increases the emotional and financial costs of the proceedings.

In this particular case, we conducted a thorough assessment of my client's financial situation. We developed a realistic proposal for spousal and child support that aimed to be equitable yet favorable under the circumstances. By opting for an uncontested approach, we avoided the extensive scrutiny of his assets and the high costs associated with contested divorces, where he would have also been liable for his wife's legal fees. The strategy proved successful, and the settlement was accepted, sparing both parties the prolonged distress and expense of litigation.

In another instance, a client was inclined towards a fault divorce due to her husband's repeated infidelity. In New York, however, pursuing a fault divorce based on adultery is cumbersome and rarely advantageous, as it necessitates proving the misconduct, which then must be linked to financial claims such as marital waste. Despite the emotional drive to pursue a fault divorce, the practical implications often steer the proceedings back to no-fault grounds, focusing instead on equitable distribution without the added burden of proving fault.

These experiences underscore the importance of strategic legal planning and realistic expectations in divorce proceedings. Whether managing the expectations of high-net-worth individuals or navigating the complexities of fault versus no-fault divorces, the goal remains the same: to achieve a resolution that respects the legal rights and financial well-being of all parties involved, ideally with minimal conflict and maximum discretion.

CHAPTER 4

PROTECTING YOUR FINANCIAL INTERESTS AND YOUR ASSETS

As a professional and prominent man, safeguarding your financial interests and assets during divorce proceedings is paramount. Here, we'll explore a few strategies for asset protection, including pre and postnuptial agreements, as well as discuss the complexities of business valuation and division.

Asset protection is essential for preserving your financial well-being during divorce. There are several strategies you can employ to safeguard your assets, including:

» *Establishing a Trust:* Transferring assets to a trust can shield them from the divorce process, as they are considered separate property. Trusts can also provide additional benefits such as asset management and estate planning.

» *Maintaining Separate Accounts:* Keeping your finances separate from your spouse's can help delineate marital and non-marital assets, reducing the risk of commingling funds and simplifying asset division.

» *Implementing Asset Protection Vehicles:* Utilizing legal structures such as limited liability companies (LLCs) or family limited partnerships (FLPs) can offer an additional layer of asset protection by separating personal and business assets.

By carefully implementing these strategies, you can reduce the risk of losing valuable assets during divorce proceedings and ensure your financial security moving forward.

Pre and Postnuptial Agreements

Pre and postnuptial agreements are powerful tools for protecting your financial interests in the event of divorce. These agreements allow couples to outline the terms of asset division, alimony, and other financial matters before or during marriage, providing clarity and certainty in the event of divorce.

Pre-nuptial agreements are executed before marriage, while postnuptial agreements are executed after marriage but before divorce proceedings commence. Both types of agreements can address various financial issues, including property division, spousal support, and inheritance rights.

While pre and postnuptial agreements may not be romantic topics of discussion, they can provide invaluable protection for your financial future, particularly for individuals with significant assets or business interests.

For professionals in finance who own or have interests in businesses, navigating the complexities of business valuation and division during divorce can be challenging. Business assets are often among the most valuable marital assets, requiring careful evaluation and equitable distribution.

Business valuation involves assessing the worth of a business entity, taking into account revenue, profits, assets, liabilities, and market conditions. Once the business has been valued, the court will determine the appropriate division of assets, considering factors such as each spouse's contributions to the business, future earning potential, and financial needs.

Navigating business valuation and division requires expertise in both finance and family law. Consulting with financial experts and experienced attorneys can help ensure that your business interests are accurately valued and fairly divided, protecting your financial interests throughout the divorce process.

Divorce Decoded

CHAPTER 5

EQUITABLE DISTRIBUTION AND ASSET DIVISION

Equitable distribution lies at the heart of divorce proceedings in New York, shaping the division of marital assets and liabilities. In this chapter, we'll delve into the principles of equitable distribution laws, explore the factors considered in asset division, and discuss strategies for negotiating property settlements.

New York follows the principle of equitable distribution, which means that marital property is divided fairly but not necessarily equally. This differs from community property states where assets are divided equally.

Equitable distribution takes into account various factors such as the length of the marriage, each spouse's financial contributions, earning capacity, and future needs. The goal is to achieve a distribution that is fair and just given the circumstances of the case.

It's important to note that equitable distribution applies only to marital property, which generally includes assets acquired during the marriage. Separate property, such as assets owned before the marriage or received as gifts or inheritances, are typically not subject to division.

Understanding equitable distribution laws is essential for advocating for your fair share of marital assets and liabilities during divorce proceedings.

When dividing marital assets and liabilities, the court considers a wide range of factors to determine what distribution is equitable under the circumstances. Some of the key factors include:

Duration of the marriage;

Income and earning capacity of each spouse;

Contributions to the marriage, including homemaking and child-rearing;

Standard of living established during the marriage;

Health and age of each spouse;

Future financial needs and circumstances; and

Any wasteful dissipation of marital assets.

By evaluating these factors, the court aims to achieve a fair and just division of assets that reflects the contributions and needs of each spouse.

Negotiating a property settlement can offer couples greater control and flexibility over the division of assets, as opposed to leaving the decision to the court. Through negotiation, spouses can work together to reach a mutually acceptable agreement that meets their respective needs and priorities.

Negotiating a property settlement involves identifying and valuing marital assets, considering tax implications, and exploring creative solutions for asset division. This may include trading assets of equal value, agreeing to retain certain assets, or structuring payment plans for equitable distribution.

Engaging in productive and transparent negotiations can help minimize conflict and expedite the divorce process, ultimately leading to a more amicable resolution for both parties.

I recall a case that perfectly illustrates the nuanced nature of equitable distribution. In this instance, my client had purchased a home before his marriage. Over the years, the value of the home appreciated significantly, largely due to his financial contributions before and during the marriage. Although the property was considered marital inasmuch as he added his wife's name to the deed, the contribution my client made was substantially greater than that of his wife.

Given the long-term nature of the marriage and considering that his wife had not been employed for most of it, we agreed on a 70-30 split of the home's equity. This decision took into account her domestic contributions—such as homemaking, which, while significant, did not financially enhance the property's value as much as my client's monetary investment did.

At one point, the decision was made to sell the home and split the proceeds according to the agreed percentage. However, as we progressed, my client reconsidered, driven by the significant value the property still held. Instead of selling, we opted for an appraisal. After deducting the outstanding mortgage and accounting for my client's initial investment, we calculated the net equity to be divided between them.

Ultimately, my client decided to buy out his wife's share, paying her 30% of the home's current equity. He managed to secure the funds through family support, specifically from a property sale his mother had recently concluded. This option allowed him to retain the home without needing a secondary mortgage, showcasing a flexible approach to resolving such disputes.

This case highlights not only the flexibility within the framework of New York's equitable distribution laws but also the importance of transparency and strategic financial planning in divorce proceedings. The ability to adapt to changing circumstances and the client's needs is crucial in achieving fair outcomes that respect both parties' contributions and future financial stability.

CHAPTER 6

ALIMONY, MAINTENANCE, AND SPOUSAL SUPPORT

Navigating the complexities of alimony and spousal support can be daunting, especially for professional men in finance facing divorce. Alimony, also known as spousal support or maintenance, is financial assistance provided by one spouse to the other during and/or after divorce proceedings. In New York, there are several types of alimony arrangements:

» ***Temporary Alimony*** also referred to as *pendente lite* support, is awarded during the divorce process to provide financial support to the dependent spouse until a final settlement is reached.

» ***Permanent Alimony*** may be awarded in cases where one spouse is financially dependent on the other and requires ongoing support after the divorce is finalized. However, true "permanent" alimony is becoming less common, and instead, courts often opt for durational or rehabilitative alimony.

» ***Durational Alimony*** provides financial support for a specific period, typically based on the duration of the marriage. It is designed to help the recipient spouse transition to financial independence.

» ***Rehabilitative Alimony*** is awarded to support the recipient spouse while they undergo education or training to become self-sufficient. It is intended to enable the recipient spouse to acquire the skills or credentials necessary to re-enter the workforce or improve their earning capacity.

Each type of alimony serves a specific purpose and may be awarded based on the unique circumstances of the case.

When determining alimony awards, New York courts consider a variety of factors to ensure fairness and equity. Some of the key factors include:

Duration of the marriage
Income and earning capacity of each spouse
Age and health of each spouse
Standard of living established during the marriage
Contributions to the marriage,
including homemaking and child-rearing

Financial needs and circumstances of each spouse

By evaluating these factors, the court aims to establish an alimony arrangement that enables the dependent spouse to maintain a standard of living similar to that enjoyed during the marriage while also considering the financial resources and obligations of the paying spouse.

Life circumstances can change following divorce, necessitating modifications to alimony orders. In New York, either party can petition the court for a modification of alimony if there has been a substantial change in circumstances, such as:

Loss of employment or reduction in income
Disability or illness preventing the paying spouse from fulfilling their alimony obligations
Remarriage or cohabitation of the recipient spouse

Modifying alimony orders requires demonstrating to the court that the change in circumstances justifies an adjustment to the existing alimony arrangement. It's essential to consult with an experienced attorney to navigate the process effectively and advocate for your interests.

Understanding the nuances of alimony and spousal support can empower you to navigate the divorce process with confidence and clarity. By prioritizing the well-being of your children and advocating for their financial security, you can navigate the challenges of divorce with compassion and resilience.

Spousal support is one of the most complex and emotionally charged aspects of divorce proceedings. It's crucial to approach these matters strategically from the start to ensure fair outcomes for all parties involved. I always advise beginning with a clear number in mind for temporary support and adjusting as necessary as the case progresses.

In one notable case, I represented a client whose spouse had significantly lower earnings but had made substantial domestic contributions, allowing my client to ascend professionally. Despite the income disparity, the court deemed it just to award him spousal support after considering his role in supporting my client's career. The temporary support was recalculated at the end of the divorce, and we managed to negotiate a reduced sum for the remainder of the support period, which was settled in a lump sum payment. This approach not only simplified the process but also minimized potential tax implications.

Another scenario involved negotiating indirect spousal support payments. Instead of direct monthly payments, my client supported his ex-spouse by covering her significant living expenses, including rent and costs related to their children. This arrangement was financially advantageous and allowed for potential tax benefits, demonstrating the flexibility available in structuring spousal support.

A particularly interesting case involved a high-net-worth individual whose ex-spouse initially sought a high amount of alimony. Upon a detailed review of her finances, it was revealed she had substantial savings and a viable professional license, suggesting she could re-enter the workforce. Leveraging this information, we negotiated a significantly reduced support arrangement for a limited period, allowing her time to transition back to employment without undue financial strain on my client.

In this case, by highlighting her financial stability and professional capabilities, we were able to save my client an estimated $200,000 in potential spousal support and associated housing costs. This outcome not only provided fair financial support for his ex-spouse but also protected my client's financial interests, illustrating the importance of thorough financial investigations and strategic negotiations in divorce cases.

These examples underscore the importance of detailed financial scrutiny and creative legal strategies in determining spousal support. Each case is unique, and a tailored approach ensures that the outcomes are equitable, taking into account the diverse contributions and needs of both parties involved.

CHAPTER 7

CHILD SUPPORT AND CHILD CUSTODY

As a professional man in finance navigating divorce, ensuring the well-being and financial security of your children is paramount. In this chapter, we'll provide an accessible overview of child support guidelines in New York, explore the determination of child custody arrangements, and discuss parenting plans and co-parenting strategies to foster a supportive environment for your children during and after divorce.

Child support is a crucial aspect of divorce proceedings, intended to ensure that children receive the financial support they need to thrive. In New York, child support is determined based on state-mandated guidelines, which take into account factors such as:

Each parent's income and earning capacity
The number of children requiring support
Childcare expenses
Healthcare costs
Educational expenses
Extracurricular activities

These guidelines provide a framework for calculating child support payments, helping to ensure consistency and fairness in support arrangements. It's essential to familiarize yourself with these guidelines to understand your rights and obligations regarding child support.

Child custody arrangements can vary widely depending on the circumstances of each family. Here are some examples of custody arrangements:

» *Shared/Joint Physical Custody:* Sarah and David, despite their divorce, have an amicable relationship and decide to share physical custody of their children. The children spend alternating weeks with each parent, allowing them to maintain close relationships with both parents.

» *Primary Physical Custody with Parenting Time:* Mark and Emily agree that it's in their children's best interests for Emily to have primary physical custody. The children reside primarily with Emily, but Mark has regular parenting time rights, including weekends and holidays, ensuring that he remains an active presence in their lives.

» *Joint Legal Custody with Sole Physical Custody:* Mike and Laura decided that while Laura will have sole physical custody of their children due to logistical reasons, they will share joint legal custody. This means that both parents have an equal say in important decisions regarding their children's upbringing, such as education and healthcare.

» *Sole Custody with Supervised Parenting Time:* In cases where one parent is deemed unfit or poses a risk to the children's well-being, the court may award sole custody to the other parent with supervised parenting time for the non-custodial parent. For example, if a parent has a history of substance abuse or domestic violence, supervised parenting time may be necessary to ensure the children's safety.

Determining child custody arrangements involves considering various factors, including the child's best interests, parental capabilities, and the existing parent-child relationship. It's essential to prioritize the child's well-being and work collaboratively to establish a custody arrangement that meets their needs.

Parenting plans are detailed agreements outlining how parents will share responsibilities and make decisions regarding their children's upbringing. These plans typically address:

Parenting time schedules and arrangements
Holiday and vacation schedules
Communication protocols between parents
Methods for resolving disputes and conflicts
Responsibilities for decision-making regarding the child's upbringing

Effective co-parenting strategies emphasize open communication, mutual respect, and a focus on the child's best interests. By prioritizing collaboration and cooperation, parents can create a supportive and stable environment for their children, even during divorce.

Child support and child custody are areas of family law that require careful consideration of numerous factors, including each parent's earning capacity, the number of children, and various child-related expenses. In my practice, I've dealt with a range of scenarios that highlight the complexities involved in these cases.

In one case, I represented a client who, due to his demanding job and travel schedule, knew he wouldn't be able to manage joint residential custody. Acknowledging this early on allowed us to negotiate a reasonable child support payment that deviated from the standard guidelines to better fit the needs of his children living in New York City. This proactive approach helped avoid prolonged disputes and ensured the children's financial needs were met without unnecessary conflict.

Another client faced challenges with joint legal custody due to his limited availability to make timely decisions about his children's lives. To address this, we arranged "spheres of influence," where he had the final say over educational matters, while the mother had control over medical and religious decisions. This setup reduced contention by allowing both parents to have authority in specific areas of their children's lives, fostering a cooperative environment despite their differences.

I also handled a case involving sole legal custody, where continuous disagreements between the parents significantly affected their child's well-being. The father's refusal to cooperate on essential health decisions led the court to grant the mother sole legal custody, emphasizing the child's best interests over parental disagreements.

Regarding supervised parenting time, I represented a father who lost significant custody rights due to his inability to cooperate with the mother and his denial of the child's medical needs. The court limited his parenting time to non-consecutive days, highlighting the serious consequences of failing to collaborate in co-parenting.

Lastly, modifications of child support and custody orders can be crucial as circumstances change. I had a client who failed to update his support order as his child aged, resulting in overpayments for childcare and tutoring not applicable to an older child. This oversight led to a contentious dispute over payments that were no longer appropriate, underscoring the importance of timely modifications to reflect current needs and capabilities.

These cases illustrate the dynamic nature of family law, where tailored solutions and proactive legal strategies are essential to protect the interests of the children and ensure fairness for all parties involved.

CHAPTER 8

THE DIVORCE PROCESS IN NEW YORK

In this chapter, we'll explain the process of filing for divorce, discuss the discovery process, and explore mediation and settlement negotiations as alternative dispute resolution methods.

Filing for divorce in New York typically involves the following steps:

» *Meet the Residency Requirements:* Before filing for divorce in New York, either you or your spouse must meet the state's residency requirements. Generally, you or your spouse must have lived in New York for at least one year before initiating divorce proceedings, unless specific exceptions apply.

» *Choose the Grounds for Divorce:* New York allows for both fault-based and no-fault grounds for divorce. *No-fault divorce* is based on the irretrievable breakdown of the marriage, while a *Fault-based divorce* requires proving marital misconduct such as adultery, cruelty, or abandonment.

» *File and Serve the Divorce Papers:* To initiate divorce proceedings, you'll need to file a summons and complaint or summons with notice with the appropriate court in your county. Once filed, you must serve copies of the divorce papers to your spouse, who then has the opportunity to respond.

» *Negotiate a Settlement or Litigate:* After filing for divorce, you and your spouse will have the opportunity to negotiate a settlement agreement addressing key issues such as asset division, child custody, and support. If you're unable to reach an agreement, the case may proceed to litigation, where a judge will make decisions on contested issues.

» *Finalize the Divorce Decree:* Once all issues are resolved, either through settlement or trial, the court will issue a final divorce decree, formally ending the marriage.

Understanding the divorce filing process can help you navigate the legal proceedings with confidence and efficiency, ensuring that your rights and interests are protected throughout the process.

During divorce proceedings, both parties have the right to gather information and evidence relevant to the case through a process known as discovery. The discovery process may involve:

» *Document Production*: requesting documents such as financial records, bank statements, tax returns, and employment records.

» *Interrogatories*: submitting written questions to the other party, which must be answered under oath.

» *Depositions*: conducting sworn testimony under oath, typically in the presence of attorneys and a court reporter.

The discovery process allows parties to gather essential information to support their case and ensure full transparency and disclosure between spouses.

Mediation and settlement negotiations offer alternative dispute resolution methods for resolving divorce-related issues outside of court. In mediation, a neutral third-party mediator facilitates discussions between spouses to help them reach a mutually acceptable agreement on contested issues. Settlement negotiations involve direct communication between spouses or their attorneys to negotiate the terms of a settlement agreement.

Both mediation and settlement negotiations offer several benefits, including:

> » *Control*: Parties have greater control over the outcome and can tailor agreements to meet their unique needs and priorities.
> » *Privacy*: Proceedings are confidential, minimizing public exposure and maintaining privacy.

» ***Cost-Effectiveness:*** Mediation and settlement negotiations are often more cost-effective than litigation, as they typically require less time and resources.

Engaging in mediation or settlement negotiations can help parties reach amicable resolutions, reduce conflict, and expedite the divorce process.

By understanding the divorce process, you will be able to navigate divorce proceedings with confidence and clarity, ensuring the best possible outcome for yourself and your family.

Navigating the divorce process in New York involves understanding and adhering to specific legal requirements, such as residency stipulations and proper service of documents. These requirements can sometimes catch individuals off-guard, as I've seen in my practice.

I worked with a client who initially thought he didn't meet the residency requirements for filing a divorce in New York. He had moved to Chicago and wasn't sure if his intermittent stays in New York qualified him. His husband, residing overseas, complicated matters further due to their estranged relationship. Through consultation, we determined that once my client re-established sufficient residency in New York, he could file. This case underscores the importance of clear communication and legal guidance to navigate jurisdictional nuances in divorce proceedings.

Another challenging aspect of serving divorce papers occurred with a different client. His husband, anticipating the divorce, had strategically avoided accepting service by providing a non-residential address related to a mailroom facility, complicating our efforts to serve him personally as required by law. After several failed attempts and no response to follow-up communications, I filed an ex parte motion for alternative service. The court granted permission to serve the divorce papers via email, a method increasingly recognized due to its efficiency and the difficulty of serving evasive parties. This allowed us to move forward in the divorce process without further delay.

CHAPTER 9

CHOOSING AND WORKING WITH A DIVORCE ATTORNEY

In this chapter, we'll emphasize the importance of finding the right attorney, discuss building a strong attorney-client relationship, and explore efficient communication and collaboration strategies to ensure a successful partnership.

Finding the right divorce attorney is essential to navigating the complexities of the legal process with confidence and peace of mind. Here are some key reasons why choosing the right attorney matters:

» *Expertise and Experience:* A knowledgeable and experienced attorney can provide invaluable guidance and advocacy, ensuring that your rights and interests are protected throughout the divorce process.

» *Understanding Family Law:* Family law is a specialized area of practice, and it's crucial to choose an attorney who has a deep understanding of New York's family law statutes and procedures.

» *Personal Compatibility:* The attorney-client relationship is built on trust and communication. It's essential to choose an attorney with whom you feel comfortable discussing sensitive matters and who shares your goals and priorities for the case.

» **Strategic Approach:** Each divorce case is unique, and a skilled attorney will develop a strategic approach tailored to your specific circumstances and objectives, maximizing the likelihood of a favorable outcome.

Taking the time to research and interview potential attorneys can help you find the right fit for your needs and ensure that you're well-represented throughout the divorce process.

A strong attorney-client relationship is essential for effective collaboration and communication. Here are some key elements of building a successful attorney-client relationship:

» **Trust and Transparency:** Open and honest communication is essential for building trust between you and your attorney. Be forthcoming about your goals, concerns, and expectations for the case.

» *Clear Expectations:* Establish clear expectations regarding communication frequency, response times, and the attorney's role in the case. This will help ensure that both parties are aligned and working towards common goals.

» *Active Participation:* While your attorney will handle the legal aspects of the case, your active participation is crucial. Stay informed, ask questions, and provide the necessary information and documentation to support your case.

» *Respect and Professionalism:* Mutual respect and professionalism are essential components of any attorney-client relationship. Treat your attorney with respect and expect the same level of professionalism in return.

By fostering a strong attorney-client relationship based on trust, transparency, and mutual respect, you can work together effectively toward achieving your desired outcome in the divorce proceedings. Effective communication and collaboration are key to a successful attorney-client relationship. Here are some strategies for ensuring efficient communication and collaboration with your attorney:

> » *Establish Clear Channels of Communication:* Determine the best method of communication with your attorney, whether it's through phone calls, e-mails, or in-person meetings. Establish clear expectations regarding response times and availability.

> » *Stay Organized:* Keep track of important documents, e-mails, and communications related to your case. This will help ensure that you're well-prepared for meetings and discussions with your attorney.

» ***Provide Timely Feedback:*** Be proactive in providing feedback and updates to your attorney. If you have concerns or questions, don't hesitate to communicate them promptly.

» ***Follow Legal Advice:*** Trust your attorney's expertise and follow their legal advice and recommendations. Your attorney has your best interests at heart and will work diligently to achieve the most favorable outcome for your case.

By maintaining open and honest lines of communication, staying organized, and collaborating effectively with your attorney, you can navigate the divorce process with confidence and clarity, ensuring that your rights and interests are protected every step of the way.

Choosing and working with a divorce attorney is a critical decision that should not be taken lightly. It's important to find someone who not only understands the law but also aligns with your personal needs and expectations. I always emphasize to potential clients the importance of not rushing this process. It's about finding the right fit for your unique situation.

In my practice, I strive to establish a relationship built on trust and transparency from the first consultation. I often hear from clients that my approachability and relatability are what draw them to choose and stay with our firm. I believe in being upfront about the divorce process, the costs involved, and what each client can expect in terms of communication and case management.

For instance, I had a client, "Client Green," who initially worked with me and appreciated our firm's approach. However, due to financial constraints, he decided to look for a less expensive option. After a year of frustration and inadequate representation, he struggled to find another attorney who matched the level of service and personal attention our firm provided. He returned to our office, expressing regret over his decision to leave in the first place. We were able to reestablish our working relationship, and I took on his case once again, this time to modify his custody order amidst challenging circumstances with his ex-wife.

This experience highlights a common pitfall—choosing an attorney based solely on cost without considering how the attorney-client relationship and the firm's communication strategies might impact the outcome of your case. It's essential to ask detailed questions about billing practices, and communication methods. At our firm, clients can schedule meetings at their convenience, communicate through a dedicated portal, and receive regular updates, which ensures that they are well informed and comfortable throughout the process.

Ultimately, the key to a successful attorney-client relationship in divorce proceedings is finding someone who not only has the requisite legal expertise but also values transparency and invests in their clients' well-being. This approach has not only led to successful outcomes but has also built lasting trust with my clients, who know they can rely on our firm during such a pivotal time in their lives.

CHAPTER 10

POST-DIVORCE
CONSIDERATIONS AND
CONCLUSION

Congratulations! You've successfully navigated the divorce process and emerged on the other side. As you embark on this new chapter of your life, it's essential to consider several post-divorce considerations to ensure a smooth transition and secure your future. Adjusting to life after divorce can be a challenging and emotional journey, but it's also an opportunity for growth, self-discovery, and new beginnings. Here are some strategies for navigating this transition:

» *Give Yourself Time to Heal.* Divorce is a significant life change, and it's okay to take time to grieve the loss of your marriage. Allow yourself to experience a range of emotions and seek support from friends, family, or a therapist.

» *Focus on Self-Care.* Prioritize self-care and wellness as you navigate this transition. Take care of your physical, emotional, and mental well-being by engaging in activities that bring you joy, relaxation, and fulfillment.

» *Rediscover Your Passions.* Use this opportunity to rediscover your interests, hobbies, and passions. Explore new activities, set personal goals, and focus on building a fulfilling and meaningful life post-divorce.

› *Establish a Support System.* Surround yourself with supportive friends, family members, and professionals who can offer encouragement, guidance, and perspective as you adjust to life after divorce.

Remember, adjusting to life after divorce is a process, and it's okay to take things one day at a time. Be patient with yourself, practice self-compassion, and trust that with time, you'll find your footing and create a fulfilling and rewarding life post-divorce. As you transition into life post-divorce, it's crucial to update your legal documents to reflect your new marital status and ensure that your wishes are properly documented and protected. Some essential documents to update may include:

» *Healthcare Proxy and Power of Attorney:*
Update your healthcare proxy and power of
attorney documents to designate new
individuals to make medical and financial
decisions on your behalf if needed.

» *Beneficiary Designations:* Review and
update beneficiary designations on retirement
accounts, life insurance policies, and other
financial accounts to ensure that they align
with your current wishes and circumstances.

» *Real Estate Titles and Deeds:* Update
property titles and deeds to reflect any
changes in ownership or distribution of real
estate assets resulting from your divorce. By
updating these legal documents, you can
ensure that your wishes are properly
documented and that your assets and affairs
are managed according to your preferences,
providing peace of mind and protection for
yourself and your loved ones.

In a particularly challenging post-judgment divorce matter, I had the privilege of assisting a client with issues that arose from the original divorce decree, involving both custody and property disputes.

The first issue concerned custody. The father was not complying with the agreed-upon terms, specifically his refusal to engage with a parent coordinator, which was crucial for managing ongoing disputes. By adhering strictly to the step-by-step process outlined in the custody order, we addressed the issue without needing to escalate to court. We sent detailed correspondence outlining the problem, provided him with the option to work with the parent coordinator, and clarified the consequences of non-compliance. Ultimately, our methodical approach paid off, and he agreed to participate in the coordination process, which greatly relieved my client.

`The second issue was more intractable and related to a piece of marital property—specifically, land that was supposed to have been sold, with my client receiving her share of the proceeds. Unfortunately, her ex-husband was dragging his feet and failed to comply with this part of the decree. In response, I filed an emergency motion to address this defiance. The court ruled in our favor, not only compelling him to proceed with the sale but also ordering him to cover my client's legal fees for having to bring this motion. This decision not only resolved the property issue but also reimbursed her for the unnecessary legal expenses incurred due to her ex-husband's non-compliance.

My client was immensely pleased with the outcome, as we managed to resolve both issues effectively, one through negotiation and the other through legal intervention. This experience underscores the importance of a meticulous approach to post-judgment issues and reaffirms my commitment to advocating for my client's rights and well-being long after the initial verdict.

As you reach the end of this journey, I want to offer my final thoughts and encouragement to you. Divorce is undoubtedly a challenging and often emotionally fraught process, but it's also an opportunity for growth, resilience, and new beginnings. Remember that you are not alone in this journey. Seek support from trusted friends, family members, or professionals who can offer guidance, encouragement, and perspective as you navigate the complexities of divorce and adjust to life afterward. Above all, remember to be gentle with yourself and allow yourself grace as you transition into this new chapter of your life. You are stronger and more resilient than you realize, and with time, patience, and perseverance, you will emerge from this experience stronger, wiser, and more empowered. Moving forward, embrace the opportunities for growth and self-discovery that lie ahead of you. Trust in your ability to create a life filled with joy, fulfillment, and purpose, and know that brighter days are on the horizon.

Thank you for allowing me to accompany you on this journey. Wishing you strength, resilience, and boundless happiness in all your future endeavors.

With warmest regards,
Asia Scarlett-Jones

Author Bio

Asia Scarlett-Jones, Esq. is the founder and managing attorney of ASJ Law Office, a law firm dedicated to providing personalized representation to clients during their most challenging moments. Established to offer individualized support, the ASJ Law Office understands that the legal system can be intimidating and overwhelming. With a commitment to guiding clients through these complexities, Asia Scarlett-Jones ensures that clients feel supported and empowered throughout the process.

About ASJ Law Office

At ASJ Law Office, clients can rest assured that they are not alone in navigating change. Whether facing financial planning or embroiled in emotionally draining divorce and custody disputes, the team at ASJ Law Office is here to help. If you need assistance, please get in touch with the ASJ Law Office at 929-600-2659.

Made in the USA
Columbia, SC
15 September 2024

41766352R00057